Bugs have Us Surrounded

Poems by Mark Wekander
Illustrations by MaryAnn Mackinnon

Bugs have Us Surrounded

Copyright 2013
Text by Mark Wekander
Illustrations by MaryAnn Mackinnon
All rights reserved.
ISBN 978-0-9849447-2-9

Published by Rubber Tree Books
111 Calle Washington 4
San Juan, Puerto Rico 00907

Cover Design by MaryAnn Mackinnon

Table of Contents

The following poems have been previously published.

Termite Cycle, published in *Stickman Review*
Lightning Bugs, published in *Edgez*

Bugs have Us Surrounded

God said, "People earth,"
some say, but truth is
it was already bugged.
We have reached 7 billion
but so many insects
outnumber us. Ants,
flies, bees and termites,
to name a few, beat us
a billion to one. To be
in the plain majority
we form small colonies
on uninhabitable Antarctica.

Now the news says
that as we knock off
other plants and animals
from the globe, we turn
to new prey to feed
seven-billion growling
stomachs with locust, mealy
bugs, termites, crickets,
cicadas, larvae, and locust.
Entomophagy will be the rage.
Already unknowingly we eat
a pound a year of insect parts,
processed in chocolate, peanut butter,
and canned food, said the FDA.
Now chocolate will cover ants,
peanut butter fill grasshopper
hors d'oeuvres, and worms
spice up stir fries and bug loaf.

The thousand flies that once
turned our limbs to dirt,
the termites that clear forest floors,
the cicadas that drum the night,
all of these will fuel our kind
which will come to an end
when we exhaust all else edible.

Calling the Bugs

Names misrepresent insects,
caught in verbal resin
and willy-nilly nomenclature.
No one has coined a name
cockroaches will answer to.
Scream roach, *cucaracha*, *kakkelakker*
and they flee, furious and disgusted,
sulking in kitchen crevices.

The hornet, elegantly figured,
an hour-glass, a string of beads,
will not be pacified by invocation.
What use is our febrile search
for the next nameable entomoid
if they're annoyed or ignore the names?

Whatever name you use to tell
the aphid to be gone is wrong.
A chewing beetle won't miss a bite
despite our pleas that he or she desist.
How many of us have prayed,
mosquito, get, oh get away
and heard only a dumb buzzing.

Termite Cycle

What sends throngs against light,
dancing their damn wings off?
Phantoms battle for the light,
dark clumsy wing-work.
With cocoons, a dressing room
is needed when the grub grows
wings, from larva to butterfly.
But to drop them, the termite,
if anyone is watching, does
a public metamorphosis.
In the morning waspish wings litter
the floor below the bulb,
costumes tossed like hot cars
ditched after the job. But this
is prior to the mayhem.
Wingless angels of decay,
they worm off somewhere
dark, bore a table leg, a fallen branch,
drill a Bible from 'b' to back,
knocking out letters like a primitive
computer virus. "Thou shall not
ommit adultery." "Though I walk
in the alley of death, I fear no evil."
"Love thy neighbor as thy elf."
Decay brings the New Age.
And after chewing through
Kant, boring *Finnegan's*
Wake, and ingesting *The Joy*
Of Cooking, once again
clumsy dancers fly the night,
the new degeneration.

Fire-Ant Hills

A
short-fused
gossip mill reddish
brown hate spreads—
like oil spills, coffee boiling over.

Fire
ants drill
and burn, twist nerves.
Red heads thread a net,

hot
pain, hot-
throb, hot itch.

Hills
pop up
and turn my yard
to acne, no dermatologist

for
fire-ant
land mines,
to latent-pain pockets

teeth
that wait
to be pulled
out of nowhere.

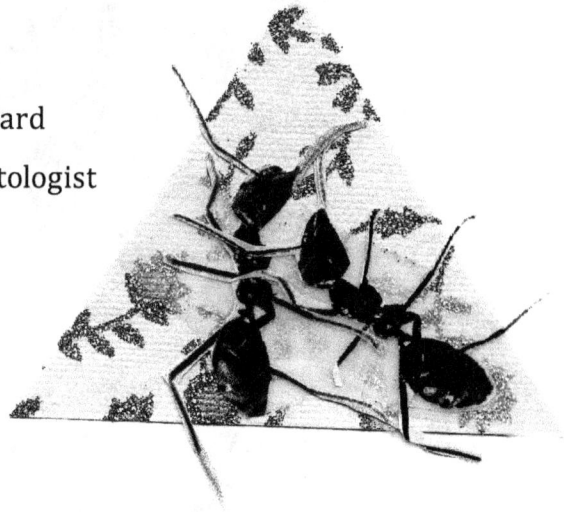

Dragonflies

Dragonflies bounce sunlight
black-green metal metaphors
of memory, winged like a Greek
trireme, oars splashing light
over rocks in a river pool

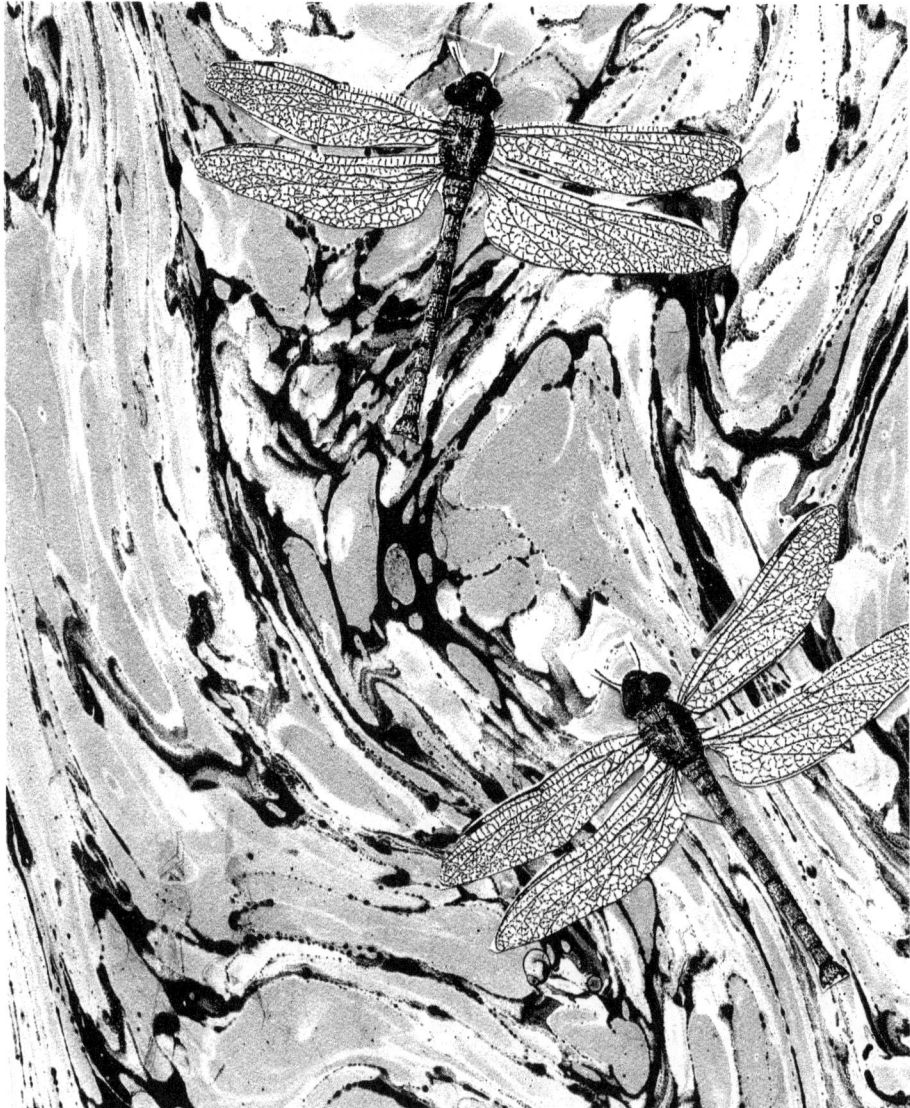

The Envious Helicopters

If only I like the damsel fly
could hover elegantly, wings
in double sets, spellbind by grace,
and not be a long-tailed-pig
grunting its belly up from dust.

Love Bugs

Indecent sex-crazed
windshield slime
too screwed and screwing to fret
truck grills, bird beaks,
lizard tongues, given to the moment
which seems to last forever
compared to peacocks who rustle feathers,
fibrillate Busby Berkeley syncopation,
put their passion in their foreplay
and then after vain male display
it's hop and pop the peahen.

No, love bugs chug love
up water-logged Louisiana summer.
They cleave to each other, even
as death speeds down I-10.
Mating is a group sport,
as if a coliseum's fans
were spectators and inspected.
With careful balance they avoid
while pairing the pairing near them.
There's no privacy like passion's blinds.
And who's the she and who isn't
isn't clear, and less so
as windshield slime dries.

Caculos – Puerto Rican May Bugs

The Grub

May-bug grubs, subterranean slugs,
white bag-thick skin. The heads,
brown clawless nails,
burrow spaghetti mansions.
They are loners, who dig subways.
When shovels and hoes, rude
intruders, turn them to the world,
the *caculo* grubs curl up demurely.

The Beetle

Caculos - round, brown, and dull,
lazy buzzing popcorn, churned
from dirt, turned from root
to nocturnal leaf plague - munch banana leaves
to the main vein, strip the moca tree
so it survives on leaf spines,
combs sunlight, and stunts.

Voracious turtles of the air,
hard shells, a slow go,
heads that hobble on crutch-wings,
werewolves that return to earth
to tunnels left by white thumbs.

Roach Odes

I.

Oh brother roach, I have ringed the sink
with acid powder, sprayed noxious perfume,
set up hotels with gooey floors, encouraged lizard
immigration. Now for several days,
I have not seen you, my brother roach.
After I have brushed away the acid,
demolished the hotels, and mopped up
the perfumed spray, out of the corner
of my eye, I see your brown lacquered back
under the sink light, and underneath it
its shadow. The shoulders bulge against
the head like a body builder deformed
by muscles. Insolent and sullen at once,
you, my brother, wait for me to move,
then you and your shadow run before
I can smash the two to one.

II.

On Magazine Street in New Orleans I lived
in a small apartment in a vivisected mansion
that butted up against the Irish Channel.
There at night, millions of spiritless souls,
which resembled hoards of roaches, filed out
from between the loose slats and grooves
of the kitchen walls and sauntered 'til dawn.

III.

Oh New York City, the capital of cockroaches!
Not the flyers or the size of the tropical roach,
but more prolific than rabbits, as fleet as
leopards' feet, and famed for eating all
from soap to the yellow glue that binds books.

In New York one can never be totally alone
with walls, drawers and crevices crowded so.
One knows they are there, even though
New York roaches can be so swift
you need faith to believe they exist.

Flies 1

Flies on the Screen

Leotard tights—
black cinematic anthro-fly thighs.
Black garden-hose tongues
go sexwire, haywire.

Steeped in malevolence
on maggot-colored screens,
devoid of garbage pail decay,
they possess procreating malaise.

Sleep has its own movie screen:

a flat wall where the world ends.

Flies 2

At the Windowsill

I wake to massacres weeks old—
flies fallen tapping Morse
on glass. Warped wings buzzed code.
Now black cadavers punctuate
the sill and lizards
trounce body debris.
Blue-bottles glisten like lures,
buzz against the glassy River Styx.

Flies 3

Still at the Sill

1

Black coated squat men
nap on the white narrow board,
 too weary to care.
After circling evasions,
now not wary of where they are,
here on the edge of the world.
If they open their eyes,
they can see it all,
but air is a smooth wall.
And they are tired of looking
at what won't welcome them.

2

Death engorged them.
Silence shrunk the universe.
It cushioned desiccated corpses.
Flies on this celestial screen sleep.
Death is life's photo negative.
Their wings spread like white robes.

Flies 4

The Hero

Why not busy as a fly?
They loop the loop,
dive bomb, dash,
get there, get back.
They're winged black boilers,
athletic energy machines.
Always a wing beyond
the swatter. "Got her?" "No."
They fly through horse-tail hail,
make food raids in foggy Raid,
brave snake, frog, and lizard tongues.
Cavalier in diet, chantilly *crème*
and excrement spice their lives.
Weak hearts faint where they thrive.
Bombers, they notch missions on the throttle,
and the blue-bottle black-dots the world,
each shit a mission accompli.

Footnote to Heroes

Thank God flies
don't shit on the wing
like planes and starlings.
Instead to evacuate,
they punctuate.

Webs

Hurricane doilies twirl
air and ocean.
We, the miniscule spots on radar,
await rain bullets shot
from a wind barrel,
cluster to targets,
our hearts dark red pools
in the lull of a bull's eye.

Spiders live in broken circles
believe in wholeness
and meaning, hang starlight
from feathery strands,
catch pieces and moments.

Tuned to galactic templates,
they churn constellations
at arachnidan pace
spin twilight, enlace night,
leaves, flowers, and winds
in the shroud's soul light.
Their nets cull black spots of life.

Butterflies

¡Es de noche...ya no hay mariposas!
                Manuel Gutierrez Nájera

Mariposas, flowers of the air,
Gutiérrez Nájera wrote an ode
to you, in bound wings that I
translated wrong years ago.
To him, you were enamel
in the air, souls of roses, coquets
and flighty women who swung
in leafy hammocks. And well,
you were tenuous life,
lit by sun rays, put out
by rain, shadows and night.

Everyone does butterflies.
Why who can resist
their Cinderella-ugly-duckling tale,
from lowly worm to flying colors?
Its name is metaphor—not,
but like something else—
        not a fly, or summer bird,
or gaudy curtain wings that flit
with peripatetic joy, mother
        of a worm, child of a worm,
a worm morphed to angel,
wings sprayed with powder,
snipped out with scissors,
flying flowers, flower on flower.

Back then, I could not translate

Gutiérrez Nájera; all his words
were romance and soul, a net,
of imagination with gaping holes,
that I crammed as best I could
to sense. He saw no Pygmalion
or an insect of the phylum
insectus, genus lepidoptera, instead
he bejeweled his words
like Huysman's turtle, until
there was no butterfly at all,
just lost love, ephemeral life,
verbal flight from an endless night.

Mosquitoes

They say they like new blood,
light skin, sweat.
My clothes hamper has a halo
with up-down flight.
My pants on the hook possess
a shaky shadow,
 phlebotomists practicing drilling twill,
alight and suck to fill an abhorrent void.

I have slept under mosquito nets
and found their body-pepper
on white mesh, fan-dried.
One always gets in,
rapes me as I sleep,
inserts its member
and leaves a small pregnancy.
Its dark glutted body
satisfied, ignores mine,
hides in the corner,
waits to escape responsibility.

I have sat under cobra coils of smoke,
marinated in citronella incense.
I have blasted them with airplane propellers
but my body breaks the wind,
my back bubbles, itches.
Only one side is ever safe.

I have smashed them
to red spots and oily brown smears.
I have clapped my hands,

slammed books on the floor
newspapers on the wall
banged ankles,
twisted shoulders,
slapped ears,
slammed my nose,
bruised my legs,
stubbed my toes,
danced St. Vitas
to the drums of
self-mutilation and murder.
Success is a stain.

I have suffered,
yes, suffered welts,
itch insomnia,
prey frenzy,
offered myself lamb-like,
weary beyond the twitch and swat
of self defense,
been burned and bored
by dengue fever,
sweat soaked,
crimson-eyed,
my red blood cells
decimated, my blood
watered down to juice
the color of Pepto Bismal,
been so tired that
the energy exerted to pass
one thought lightly
through my mind

left me more dead,
the boredom, like watching
a commercial a thousand times.
I would have stopped my heart
for a moment's rest.

This is the price for knocking
fall and winter from the calendar,
for moving to the Tropics,
for having rain, having blood,
for not smelling like Off,
for not converting to poison bait
not wearing thick socks,
turtle necks, veils.

I am not new blood.
They are starving millions
and I am the only chicken in famine land.
They are voracious babes
that suck my skin and leave tiny teats.
What kind of mother am I?
Come to me my buzzing babes,
and when I see your bagpipe bellies swell,
I'll swat you on your bottoms.

Bed Bugs

Some bugs mark lines of class.
Below the bedbug lie the poor
or so it was before. Above,
not far, the middle-class boiled
sheets in steady vigilance.
My father once confessed,
after I swore an oath of silence,
that as a child, he slept
with bed bugs. His family cast
linen and mattresses out
into northeast Montana's
January cold where bed bugs
frozen dead could cloak
his grandmother's humble past.
She was a maid who married
her master's drunken son.

In pictures my father
never wears short-sleeves;
his collar clasps around his neck.
No skin with marks of shame appear.
These immigrants knew, long before
renowned sociologists, that without red
bumps and fingers on skin in fits
their poverty was just
a neighbors' social construct.

Fleas

John Donne wrote in some
metaphysical cleverness that if
the flea that bit him bit his love,
there would be some holy amorous
blend of blood, his and hers.
Not to diminish Mister Donne
or his love, but what a flea prefers
is dog blood: warmly wrapped in fur.

I know fleas in New Orleans
will take a dog any day
over tepid barely hairy humans.
But if the dogs leave, as they did
in an apartment on Dupree,
the fleas will cleave to human skin,
turn skin black below the knee
without a thought of who
the blood's previous owner was.

Some Lice

Of course, we know from childhood
that those sneaky lice are not nice.
But older, some lice change their names
to crab. Perhaps its tenacious grip
or complaining nature makes it change
its name. Not much will kill them.
Alcohol will stun them. But like
drunks, hangovers make them antsy.
Lice hang on where fleas are fickle.

And Mister Donne should know, crabs
are a surer way to mix two lovers' blood
than a flea that might have intermediarie
like rats, bears, mongoose and dogs.
As any learned historian knows,
the flea's interspecies promiscuity
can swing the scythe of mortality.

No, as insect go, crabs are not
promiscuous, but crawl from skin
to skin, slow like welfare lines,
pass from one to one and then
settle in after the lovers'
last panting race is run.

Ticks

The tick is another sucker
waiting for you to pass
through tall grass or under branches.
When young and dry, thin as
a blade of grass, it will crawl
your walls, insinuate itself below
your clothes. Then the tick
sticks its snout into skin,
using your blood like helium,
it inflates like a Macy Parade
Snoopy or Lucy. Its legs jut
from the taut body, poster
child of complete obesity.
Then filled, it becomes detached,
drops its pillowy body, and
because it's round, the legs
stick beyond the reach of ground.
Here the dimpled orb at ease
transforms your blood to progeny.

The Aphid's Attire

Aphids' bodies are not ideal
Clothed in diaphanous green.
They are rotund and cluster
 like grapes on undersides of leaves.
Their skin provides some cover
on the leaves they suck
from ladybugs who devour
their opulent succulence
or from massacres by thumbs.

Oh, Pity the Poor Aphid

Though they make verdant life
less robust, one may the aphids pity,

when they succumb like cattle taken
in a flood, fumigated and devoured.

Even without predators and farmers,
their lives are never theirs. They are

ants' chattel, protected, yes, but herded
and bullied for their sweet feces,

and never in their tiny lives
are they just sucking for themselves.

Lightning Bugs

Fire flies, cinders float,
you are the most melancholy
insect, a sleight reminder
of childish nights, fascination.
Disjointed,
blinking memory –
the first summer
I was astounded
by humid night bejeweled.
We de-lighted bugs.
Sticky ectoplasm bound light
to our fingers, foreheads.
We children wed night,
firefly rings and diadems,
Milky Way trains, all girls
and boys brides of light.

Years later on the Delaware,
I saw the thick low-watt night,
heard light's hum-hush,
life waves bobbing unconnected dots.
I was baptized, hallowed
in the river of bobbing light.
Messages floated and disappeared,
sank undeciphered into the flow.

I once saw a row of lights
and when I got close,
three lightning bugs awaited
the spider executioner.
Steadier than lightning,

cooler than fire, lazier than flies.
Their wings bore metaphors,
no chrysalis analogies:
fat indolent lightning,
cold half-hearted fire
for a flame gulping spider.

Where is lightning's blinding flash,
or envy's pulsing burn?
Lampyridae-shining tail;
those Greeks were matter-of-fact.
No lightning exaggerations,
no smoke no fire, just shine.
For the Greeks in Eden
naming was description.
The spider did not have to know
the meal's official moniker.

Some nights as I sleep
they wander my room:
the world's dying embers,
lost semaphores on a sea
whose waves lap the roof
of heaven.

Are you rehearsals
of dying stars or punctuation
of a holy text written on the night?
Cinders ignite dreams' dark flames,
burn with soft fluctuating light.

Lady Bugs

My parents are plagued
by lady beetles or lady bugs.
The Asian interlopers
cover the screen, flow
like lava from crevices,
bite red and hot, not orange,
voracious spotted Volkswagens.

They swarm and bite when
the last aphid's iced
carcass drops from the final
leaf. It's not fire they flee
in mass, but dark days
and cold nights. They are
the house on fire crackling
in winter's blue flames,
they rust, burn and bite.

Benediction from a Praying Mantis

Sibling of hypocritical politicians,
who pray for votes;
some genetically masked as twigs,
seeming inanimate to unsuspecting meals,
they are entomological etymology.
Preying and praying, bearing on
a cylindrical back the name orthopterous,
mantis, Greek for prophet, Spartan doom to the soft bodied.
(If only you would eat your fellow orthopterous –
cockroaches, crickets, and the grasshopperous.)

Splinter of log cabin homeliness
petrified to hide fierce jaws,
lanky, bats bashing beetles,
joyless impersonator of the impersonal,
symbol of the resurrected twig,
fallen and moving, uncrossed,
patient agent that vanishes rounder earths,
bless us with fake surplus penitence.
Metaphor of deception, praying and preying,
"for the world which seems to lie before us like a"
leaf or twig has legs, or to paraphrase the Cubans,
cada persona es un mundo - each creature is a world,
in the infinite minutia, like humans
whose heavenly bodies come to earth,
grow arms and legs to run from dust,
brilliant to the infrared, more twig-like
than star-like. Deceivers to achieve dinner,
bless us the wearers of elaborate deception.

The Breeding of the Carolina Mantis

Who doesn't understand the maid
at forty-eight who confessed
to having heard a rumor that
if you tried sex, you were lost,
hooked on stuff harder than crack?
We who have tried it and gone cold
turkey, often against our will, forget
the horrors of the last bout, or we
hunger for life's answer void of thought.

It seems that no one warns the poor
Carolina's male mantis about love,
that it can consume you, make
you lose your head, and still
keep you jumping 'til the end.
In about a fourth of the trysts
the female eats the male's head,
then gobbles up his thorax,
while his abdomen under the spell
jerks and pumps to fertilize her eggs.

So there it is, as my seventh-grade
science teacher Mrs. Undum explained,
one day when she brought her body out
of constant flux, stood stone-faced and looked
us in the eye, "Our purpose is to propagate."
And what dirty tricks hormones and nature play
to force us to participate in this soulless game.

The Internment of the Moth

In solemn silence the body
of the gray moth proceeds
across the laundry floor,
navigates around a brown
sock, a bra's tortured angles,
as if a weak magnet
drew it towards the door.
On all fours with my reading
glasses on, I crouch
to see what makes the tattered
wings and beady head progress
along so straight and steady.
The mouths of eight ant
pallbearers grip the wings
and bear the tiny casket
to the grave. Like a chance
mourner, I crawl to the hole
and watch the wings collapse
like fancy luggage, as it's pulled
headfirst into the netherworld.

The Bee Machine

A smooth motor purrs
in the royal palm's
massive head of blooms.

The Obstinacy of Bees

A queen one morning set
her palace in a speaker.
I blasted her with rock,
merengue, salsa and Mahler,
and though her subjects
were not pleased, they stayed.
Then I stoked a barbecue
with paper, wax and water
to smoke them out. A bit
dizzy, they endured the fumes.
Next I took a hose and aimed
pounding water at the hole.
They were somewhat disturbed.
Then I sprayed organic insecticide,
but her wooden castle weathered all.
The queen was safe some place
among the tinkling resonance of Bach.
Using a long pole, I unhitched
the palace from the wall
and it crashed on patio tile.
In lethargic disorder, smoke-drunk
drones twirled 'round the palace gate.
I couldn't leave the speaker
on the terrace floor, now smudged

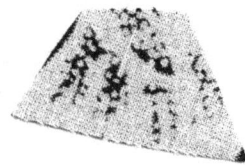

with charcoal and globs of wax
so I nudged it to a hill and let
momentum pull it down, its square
shape made it hop and jerk
until it rested on a small plateau,
where unperturbed bees buzzed
around the hole for months,
made do with their battered palace,
open to the elements, warped
by sun and rain until one day
they left upon their own accord.

Leaf Rollers

To make a bed of cucumber,
tomato, eggplant or pepper leaves
and then eat it after a good sleep
seems the ingratitude of species.

The Citrus Weevil

Oh chew, oh chew the bitter leaves
 of citrus trees in prison gangs
of two or three. Your black and off-
white jailbird stripes are armor
for your wings. Your ballpoint heads
droop, your beady eyes seem
not to see, but if a hand comes near,
you drop from half-chewed leaves
as if caught scaling the prison wall,
then make yourself scarce in weeds.

So avaricious! The female eats as
she mates, as if time were dear.
They delight in surly evil,
in destroying what others cultivate,
as they flout their snout's disdain
at the peasants' endless strain.

Those Disgusting Bugs

The insect kingdom is murderous,
with every side from matricide
to infanticide. There are grizzly
murders, serial killers like
the sinister assassin bug who inserts
a tube into his prey, embalms them
to a liquid mush, then thrusts another
like a straw and sucks up the muck.

Some mother bugs don't lay eggs
next to one another because
the first one hatched will eat
 its sisters and brothers.

Damselflies and dragonflies
have no truck with chivalry.
They do not kill with flaming tongues
or wait for heroes dressed in Franklin stoves.
No, these fancy fliers hover and dart,
then spring lower lips hinged and primed
to snap dreamers from the tranquil sky.
More mouse or bear trap than noble lance
and the force is not brawn, but more advanced.
Hydraulic power brings their prey to mouth.

Civilized, we find it hard to fathom
bugs thirsty for blood and ectoplasm.
It's rewarding to look down on
the crawling, hopping, fluttering mass
and measure how far we've advanced.

www.ingramcontent.com/pod-product-compliance
Lightning Source LLC
Chambersburg PA
CBHW051347290326
41933CB00042B/3315